Oils to the Rescue

A basic introduction to using 100% pure therapeutic grade essential oils with your pet.

Sayde Kelly C.A.M.P.
Certified Animal Massage Practitioner
Patty M Kelly

Illustrated by Matt Wayne

The information contained within this book is for educational purposes only, and only represents a guideline for your use of essential oils and products for animals. The authors will assume no liability for any loss or damage of any nature, by the use of any information contained within this publication. These statements have not been evaluated by the Food and Drug Administration. This information is not intended to treat, cure, or prevent any disease.

The authors have taken great care, to ensure that the information given in this text is accurate and up to date. Readers are strongly advised to work in cooperation with their veterinarian. Use common sense in how to proceed with any illness or administration of natural remedies.

ISBN-13:978-1547155323
ISBN-10:1547155329

Meet the Authors

Patty and Sayde are true animal advocates. Their love and passion of animals are evident in all they do. They want to share their wealth of information and training with others to assist the animal community.

In 1999 they followed their dream of owning their own business by creating Doodlebug Duds, a line of dog/cat beds, coats, collars, leashes and much more. For 18 years Doodlebug Duds has been a staple at the Portland Saturday Market.

They have partnered with a local rescue, Panda Paws Rescue, as a foster family for special needs dogs. A teeny-tiny Yorkie captured their hearts and the famous Fluffy Shark was adopted for their daughter Gerty.

A couple of years ago one of their Basset Hounds, Honey, began to exhibit severe skin issues. Multiple trips to the vet and traditional medications were not providing relief. A friend offered them a more holistic approach to the care of their pets (and themselves) 100% pure therapeutic grade essential oils. Honey found immediate relief with daily use of the oils along with her medications. Soon the entire family was using the oils on a daily basis.

In 2016 Sayde completed training through Northwest School of Animal Massage. She is now a Certified Animal Massage Practitioner (C.A.M.P.) This combined with Patty's Bachelor of Arts degree in Physical Education and Health from Pacific University, and the knowledge they have gained of the powerful benefits of 100% pure therapeutic grade oils, Patty and Sayde feel the need to share this information to help others.

PATTY GERTY FLUFFY SHARK SAYDE

Team Doodle

"Meet the illustrator"

Matt Wayne is an artist based in Portland Oregon. In addition to illustrating books, he is also the owner/operator of Be Good Monster, purveyor of whimsical t-shirts and shrinky dink earrings! For more information on Matt check out **www.begoodmonster.com** and find Be Good Monster on Facebook and Instagram.

"Shout out!"

We are forever grateful to Tiffin Kreger-Bryant for introducing us to these powerful essential oils. Tiffin, thank you for always believing in us, encouraging us to reach for our dreams, helping us be better versions of ourselves, and for helping us find exactly the right words.

Thank you Matt Wayne of Be Good Monster for taking these crazy concepts that we had in our heads and making them a reality for everyone to enjoy.

Thank you, Amanda Giese for showing us the world of rescue and including us in so many of your missions. We are forever grateful for your friendship and trust. You brought these animals into our world and words cannot express the impact they have had on our hearts and lives. When we met the universe aligned just right.

Thank you, Fluffy Shark (aka Doodle) for just being you.

Thank you Rhia for being such a great friend and always being there for our family.

Last, but not least, we want to thank you Gerty, our sweet, kind, beautiful, intelligent daughter. You are the perfect combination of us, logical, factual, silly and creative. Thank you for putting up with our countless hours of researching, learning, studying, teaching and many hours of phone calls while we were writing this book.

"Safety and precautions"

Gently introduce the oils to your pet. Diffusing is an easy way to receive the benefits of the oils and it dilutes them. Open the bottle and allow your animal to approach and sniff the oil. Notice their response. You can put the oils on your hands, rub your hands together absorbing most of the oils into your skin. Pet your animal. This allows a gentle introduction to the oil. Essential oils are safe and effective with proper use. Always consult a veterinarian for your animals care.

Start with the minimal amount and see how your animal reacts. Small frequent doses throughout the day.   Each animal's chemistry is different so the amount necessary will vary. Not all oils are created equal use only 100% pure therapeutic grade essential oils. The quality and purity of the oils is vital to your pet's health. Older animals, those with a weak immune system, and young animals need extra caution. Start with the highest dilution rate.

For the purposes of this book, we recommend only diffusing these essential oils for cats. Do not confine them to a room with a diffuser. Always allow a cat the opportunity to leave the room if they chose to.

DILUTE! DILUTE! DILUTE!
Refer to dilution chart.

As with anything new that you are introducing to yourself or your animals be watchful for any changes. For example: behavioral, skin irritations, changes in breathing, discoloration, swelling. If any of these issues occur, monitor them and call your veterinarian and temporarily discontinue use.

**As a reminder, it is not advised to ever place essential oils in ear canals, eyes or any mucus membranes.

Some oils are considered "hot" as they produce a warming sensation in their body that may cause sensitivity. A few examples of "hot" oils are: Cassia, Cinnamon, Clove, Melaleuca, Oregano, and Thyme. Dilution is recommended prior to topical application.

There are certain oils that may trigger seizures. Some of which are Rosemary, Fennel, Sage, Eucalyptus, Hyssop, and Camphor. These should be avoided with animals prone to seizures. Use essential oils with caution and always consult your veterinarian.

Dogs with bleeding disorders or difficulty clotting should avoid topical use of the following oils: Soothing Blend, Protective Blend as they contain Wintergreen, Cassia, Blue Tansy, Fennel, Clove, Cinnamon, Oregano and Sweet Birch.

Some citrus oils are photosensitive. It is best to avoid prolonged exposure to ultraviolet rays when used topically.

If it becomes necessary to remove the essential oils use a carrier oil to flush the area. DO NOT USE WATER it drives the oils in deeper.

These statements have not been evaluated by the Food and Drug administration. They are not intended to diagnose, treat, cure or prevent any disease.

"Hi, my name is Fluffy Shark, but my friends call me Doodle. I would like to share with you my family's adventures with essential oils."

I am a super cute Yorkie with a lot of attitude. I come from a rescue called Panda Paws Rescue. They mostly help special needs animals. You can learn about them at **www.pandapawsrescue.org**. When I was born I wasn't breathing. Amanda from Panda Paws breathed life into me for about 10 minutes until I was breathing on my own. Then she tube fed me until I was strong enough to eat on my own. So, do I think I am special? Absolutely!

When I turned 2 months old my new family adopted me. It was mutual love at first sight. We use essential oils every day. They help me and my people. They also help all of my furry siblings. We would like to share some of that information with you. When you are interested in joining Team Doodle and using essential oils send us an email at **teamdoodleoils@gmail.com** or go to **www.mydoterra.com/doodlebugduds**

"So, what's the deal with these essential oils?"

The use of essential oils date back to ancient times. They have been utilized throughout multiple generations, virtually every culture. They are volatile aromatic compounds from the roots, seeds, bark, stems, flowers and other parts of plants. They are pure extracts from plants and highly concentrated. We recommend the use of 100% Pure Therapeutic Grade oils only. Essential oils are safe and effective with proper use.

In the wild, when animals were left to their own accord and had health issues they would instinctively seek out the plant that had the chemical component to help restore balance in their body. Our bodies are constantly striving to be in a state of balance. We feel our best when all our systems are functioning at their optimal level. Our bodies are able to fight off infection, regulate hormones and blood pressure to run like a well oiled machine. Throughout the years we have domesticated animals. We keep dogs and cats in the house, chickens confined to their coop, horses in the barn and we feed them increasingly processed, modified foods. We have lessened their exposure to the earth and its elements, decreased their ability to seek out these oils in their natural form. All that, in addition to an ever increasing toxic environment, leads to the inability for their bodies to maintain balance. Through the use of essential oils we can now provide a natural, safe way to receive some of those same benefits.

There are 3 ways to use 100% Pure Therapeutic Grade essential oils.

Aromatically: The part of a dog's brain that is devoted to smell is 40 times greater than that of a human. Introducing essential oils to your animal can be as simple as opening the bottle. The best way to use the oils is aromatically using a diffuser. A diffuser acts as a transit system for the essential oils. It breaks them down into small particles in the air, making it easier for them to be inhaled. We recommend this as a passive way for your animals to get the benefits of the essential oils.

Topically: This is very powerful. One drop of essential oil can service every cell of your body. It nourishes your bloodstream within 30 seconds. Common locations for topical application are tips of ears, spine, belly, base of skull, large pads on back paws. Always refer to the dilution chart. (page 16) We recommend you start with the minimal amount. These oils are 100% pure and highly concentrated. A little bit goes a long way. Small frequent doses are best.

Internally: While many of these oils may be ingested, we will not be discussing internal usage.

The key to the using essential oils is small frequent doses. As with all your animal care, always consult your veterinarian. Like every person, every animal is different, therefore every essential oil experience can vary. What we are sharing with you is individual oils may work or a combination of these oils may work for your pet. Our ultimate goal is healthy, happy, thriving pets through the use of essential oils. There are many additional oils you can use effectively with your pet. This book is only addressing a few of them. This is the 1st in a series of books. Be on the lookout for future adventures with Doodle, his friends and essential oils. When you would like to learn more about these 100% Pure Therapeutic Grade essential oils contact us at: teamdoodleoils@gmail.com

Dilution ratios using essential oils on Dogs

Dog Weight	Essential Oil	Carrier Oil
0-25 lbs	1 drop	2 tbsp
26-45 lbs	1-2 drops	2 tbsp
46-75 lbs	2 drops	2 tbsp
76-90 lbs	2-4 drops	2 tbsp
90++ lbs	4 drops	2 tbsp

Always use the highest dilution ratio until you see how your pet responds to the oils. Then you can increase or decrease depending on results. Many animals require no dilution of the oils, however always dilute "hot" oils.

If your dog is close to the maximum weight, err on the side of caution and use a higher dilution ratio until you know how your dog will respond. 100% Pure Therapeutic Grade oils are very concentrated and powerful. A little bit goes a long way.

Suggested carrier oils are Fractionated Coconut Oil, Sweet Almond Oil, and Avocado Oil.

"This is where you put the oils"

*Refer to the dilution chart when necessary.

The tips of their ears: Rub 1 to 2 drops of oil in the palm of your hands, lightly rub your hands together, then wipe on the tips of your pets ears.

Base of their skull: Drop 1 to 2 drops on the base of the skull. Or put the oils in the palm of your hands, lightly rub your hands together, then wipe on the base of your pets skull.

Down their spine: Drop 1 to 4 drops of oil down my spine. Or put the oils in the palm of your hands, lightly rub your hands together, then wipe down your pets spine.

On their belly: Tap the bottle directly on my belly 1 to 3 times. Or put the oils in the palm of your hands, lightly rub your hands together, then wipe over your pets belly area.

Large pad on their back paws: Tap the bottle directly on the large pad on the back paws. Or drop 1 to 2 drops of oils in the palm of your hands, lightly rub your hands together, then wipe over the large pad on your pets back paws.

EARS

BASE OF SKULL

DOODLE

SPINE

BELLY

PADS OF FEET

Calming Oils

Cedarwood
Lavender
Frankincense
Grounding Blend
Reassuring Blend
Restful Blend
Roman Chamomile
Women's Blend

"I like lavender for car rides, it helps keep me calm"

Lavender is known for its calming and relaxing qualities. It has been used as far back as ancient Egyptian and Roman times for these very reasons. Lavender is considered a must have oil to keep on hand due to its versatile uses.

Recommended application: 1 to 2 drops in the palm of your hands, rub your hands lightly together and put it on the tips of their ears and along their spine. 1 to 2 drops of oil on a cotton ball can be placed in the air vent to act as a diffuser if you don't have a car diffuser. This allows for a more relaxed ride to a new home, the vet office, or a trip to the park.

Alternative oils: Roman Chamomile, Reassuring Blend, Restful Blend, Grounding Blend, Frankincense, Cedarwood

"Dude, I don't know what it is about that Restful Blend and the volcano, but I like it."

Diffusing essential oils is a great way for you and your pets to aromatically receive them throughout the day and night. The diffuser works by distributing essential oil molecules through the air. Once in the air, they are inhaled. Depending upon which oils you are diffusing, they assist your body in achieving the desired effect. Restful Blend is a combination of several oils. Lavender, Roman Chamomile, Vetiver and Cedarwood to name a few. Along with other oils their calming and relaxing qualities make a powerful combination. Because of these qualities, these oils have a long historical use in various cultures.

Recommended applications: Place 3 to 4 drops of oil in the diffuser. Put 1 to 3 drops in the palm of your hands, rub your hands together lightly and wipe down their spine and tips of ears. Put 1 to 2 drops on your pet's bandana or collar.

Alternative oils: Lavender, Roman Chamomile, Cedarwood, Frankincense, Grounding Blend, Women's Blend, Reassuring Blend

"SQUIRREL!!"

Calming your wild beast can be difficult. The Women's Blend is a combination of oils specifically designed to provide a unique scent based on your individual chemistry. However, the oils used in the Women's Blend can have a dramatic effect on your pets anxiety levels. Ylang-Ylang helps to reduce feelings of fear and anger. Jasmine calms down the body, mind and soul. Vetiver and Patchouli have a calming, grounding effect on the emotions. Vetiver has been used been used in religious ceremonies as the "fragrance of the soil".

*Refer to dilution chart
Recommended application: put 1 to 2 drops in the palm of your hands, lightly rub hands together and wipe down pets spine and on the tips of their ears. Diffuse 2 to 3 drops for a calming atmosphere or use it in advance of known stressful situations. For example: mail carrier, school's out, company, travel.

Alternative oils: Grounding Blend, Restful Blend, Lavender, Frankincense, Roman Chamomile
*or any combination of these.

"Roman Chamomile helps me feel like a brave, confident warrior while on my walk"

Roman Chamomile was used to help soldiers have courage during times of war. It has a calming effect on the body, skin and mind. It's chemical profile supports soothing the systems of the body and helps create feelings of comfort when you need them the most.

* Refer to dilution chart
Recommended application: 1 to 2 drops in the palm of your hand and wipe down your pet's spine and on the tips of their ears before their outing. Excellent oil to use for transporting scared animals or giving timid animals a boost of confidence. Diffusing 2 to 3 drops of Roman Chamomile while you are away or in your vehicle promotes feelings of relaxation. When adding it to your pets shampoo it will promote healthy looking fur and skin as well as a calming atmosphere.

Alternative oils: Lavender, Restful Blend, Grounding Blend, Reassuring Blend, Women's Blend, Frankincense

"A little help here!"

When life feels a little out of balance and a little chaotic, the Grounding Blend might be just what your pet needs. The Grounding Blend promotes tranquility while bringing harmony to the mind and body, and balance to the emotions. This blend contains Spruce Needle Oil which is known for its grounding properties; and Ho Wood Oil is excellent for promoting a peaceful and relaxing environment. It also contains Frankincense, Blue Tansy and Blue Chamomile which are all very grounding and centering oils. The chamomile plant is one of the oldest most widely used plants in the world. Known for its calming qualities and its variety of uses.

*Refer to dilution chart
Recommended application: Tap bottle on the large pad on the back paws. Place 1 to 2 drops in the palm of your hand, gently rub hands together and wipe down your pet's spine and tips of ears. Diffuse 2 to 4 drops for a calming environment. Use this blend when transporting new animals or those who are nervous traveling.

Alternative oils: Lavender, Cedarwood, Frankincense, Roman Chamomile, Restful Blend, Reassuring Blend, Women's Blend

"OHMMMM"

Anxious? Over stimulated? Lost your composure? Can't quite rein it in?
Is your pet struggling with any of these?
The Reassuring Blend may be the right combination for your pet. It contains Vetiver, Lavender and Ylang Ylang. Vetiver allows your body to restore its natural balance. Ylang Ylang helps reduce feelings of fear and anger, It also helps regulate blood pressure and hormones. Lavender is universally known for its calming qualities. This blend also contains Frankincense, which has been noted in research to help channel excessive energy and heighten concentration in those who lack focus. These oils, along with the others in the blend, promote feelings of contentment, composure and confidence.

*Refer to dilution chart
Recommended application: Place 1 to 2 drops in the palm of your hand, lightly rub hands together and wipe down your pet's spine and tips of ears. Diffuse 2 to 3 drops for a relaxed atmosphere. When transporting an anxious or timid animal this is an excellent blend to apply topically 10 minutes before travel and diffuse in your car for ongoing support.

Alternative oils: Lavender, Frankincense, Roman Chamomile, Cedarwood, Grounding Blend, Restful Blend, Women's Blend

Immune Supporting Oils
Lavender
Lemon
Melaleuca
Peppermint
Protective Blend
Respiratory Blend

"One or two drops of lavender in the tub, no more itchy skin for me!"

Lavender is calming in so many ways. Not only is it great for stress, but it helps soothe dry, irritated skin.

*Refer to dilution chart
Application: 1 to 2 drops applied directly to the skin, may dilute if necessary. Placing one to five drops in the bath water can assist in calming irritated or dry skin and allows anxious pups to learn to trust. Also excellent to use for soothing irritations caused by insect bites.

Alternative oils: Roman Chamomile, Frankincense, Cedarwood, Restful Blend

"Nothing beats a breath of fresh air"

The Respiratory Blend is a remarkable oil that helps maintain feelings of clear airways and easy breathing. The powerful combination of Peppermint, Eucalyptus, and Cardamom, along with the other oils, make this blend a must have for healthy respiratory function. In traditional Chinese medicine, Eucalyptus is known for its exceptional ability to enhance the breathing function. Peppermint oil can help clear blocked sinuses and ease nasal congestion. Cardamom, while known as a spice, is beneficial in providing relief with respiratory spasms and aids in digestive processes.

*Refer to dilution chart
Recommended application: Diffuse 2 to 4 drops. Apply 1 drop topically on the chest. Put 1 drop in the palm of your hand, lightly rub your hands together and wipe over chest area.

Alternative oils: Peppermint

"Achoooooo"

Itchy, sneezy, watery eyes. These are signs your pet's body is trying to respond to what it deems as a harmful substance. Their immune system response can cause inflammation and irritation. The combination of Peppermint, Lemon and Lavender is powerful in combating these symptoms. Peppermint Oil can help to clear blocked sinuses and ease nasal congestion. Lemon Oil helps flush toxins out of their body. Lavender helps reduce inflammatory reactions in their body.

*Refer to dilution chart

Recommended application: Apply 1 drop each of Peppermint, Lemon and Lavender 2 to 3 times a day. Apply it to their belly area or along their spine. You can also make a roller bottle of this blend (15 drops of each oil and fill the rest with fractionated coconut oil) and apply it to the large pads on their back paws 2 to 3 times a day. Diffusing these oils can provide continual support throughout the day. 1 to 3 drops of each oil in the diffuser.

Alternative oils: Respiratory Blend

"I feel as sick as a dog"

Sometimes our animals feel a little under the weather, not quite themselves for a variety of reasons. The Protective Blend has a powerful combination of oils that help boost your immune system and fight free radicals. Antioxidants help prevent free radicals from damaging your cells. Every body uses antioxidants to balance free radicals. This keeps them from causing damage to other cells, which in turn boosts your immunity. Clove, Wild Orange peel and Cinnamon oil all contain a large amount of antioxidants. These oils, combined with Eucalyptus, aids in circulation and make for a more effective immune system response.

Recommended application: Diffuse 2 to 3 drops of the Protective Blend daily for ongoing immune support.

"There is a fungus among us"

Melaleuca, also called Tea Tree oil, is known for its cleansing properties and immune support. The leaves of the Melaleuca tree have been used by the Aborigines of Australia for centuries. They used the oil for its respiratory benefits and cleansing properties.

Recommended application: Put 1 to 2 inches of water in the tub and put 1 to 3 drops of oil in the water for a foot soak.

Alternative oils: Lavender

Soothing Oils

Cedarwood
Digestive Blend
Frankincense
Lavender
Peppermint
Massage Blend
Melaleuca
Outdoor Blend
Roman Chamomile
Soothing Blend

"Oh, my aching back"

Frankincense is known as the "fix all" of the oils. This oil was used by Babylonians and Assyrians in religious ceremonies. The Egyptians used Frankincense resin for everything from perfume to soothing skin. It can be used in many different ways. Frankincense applied topically can help reduce feelings of discomfort due to inflammation. It is also used to promote feelings of peace, relaxation, and overall wellness. As the King of oils, Frankincense supports healthy cellular function.

Recommended application:1 to 3 drops on area of concern, refer to dilution chart if needed. Helps ease discomfort. Use as a proactive approach to overall wellness. Diffusing 1 to 3 drops promotes feelings of relaxation.

Alternative oils: Massage Blend, Soothing Blend, Roman Chamomile

"Protective shield activated"

What better way to combat nature then with nature itself. The Outdoor Blend is a combination of nature's finest offerings to combat unwanted intruders. This blend includes Cedarwood and Arborvitae which are widely known as natural insect repellants. Historically Arborvitae is called the "tree of life" and was used by Native Americans for its natural preserving properties, building vessels and creating totem poles.

Recommended application: This blend is prediluted. You can use 1 to 3 drops neat down the spine and belly of your pet. You can put 1 to 3 drops in the palm of your hands, lightly rub them together and wipe down your pet's spine. Put 10 drops in a 4 ounce glass spray bottle, fill the rest with water, shake mixture, and spray on pet's body. Excellent to use on humans as well. Diffuse this blend for an outdoor/indoor insect repellant. Apply topically on new pets for transport and play dates.

Alternative oils: Cedarwood

"I can't stop scratching my ears"

Melaleuca, also called tea tree oil, is well known for its ability to provide relief and rejuvenation to irritated skin. It is used in many skin care products because of its cleansing and soothing properties. The shape of your pet's ear canal makes it the perfect breeding ground for moisture. Melaleuca has been used to fight against yeast infections due to its powerful properties.

*Refer to the dilution chart
Recommended application: 1 to 2 drops of oil on a cotton ball and wipe out their ears. *DO NOT ENTER THE EAR CANAL. If possible leave the cotton ball in their ears for approximately 5 minutes.   Put 1 drop on the tips of your pointer finger and place your finger at the opening of the ear canal and do a very gentle pulsating massage. This acts as a diffuser for the oils. *DO NOT ENTER THE EAR CANAL. Place 1 to 2 drops on a cotton ball and wipe around the external base of your pets ears. Doodle tip: A proactive measure we use, is continued use.

Alternative oils: Frankincense and Lavender
*these are to be in addition to Melaleuca

"When my bro Bowy and I get a little too wild it's Soothing Blend to the rescue"

Whether it is a specific muscle that is sore or an overall tense feeling, the Soothing Blend may be just what you need. It contains a variety of oils that aid in soothing sore muscles and increasing circulation. Some of which are Peppermint, Ylang Ylang, Helichrysum and Blue Chamomile. Helichrysum has been widely studied for its health benefits, notably its effect on inflammation and blood flow. Soothing Blend with a proper dilution can be part of a cooling and comforting massage for your dog.

*Refer to dilution chart
Recommended application: 1 to 2 drops of oil in the palm of your hand, lightly rub hands together and wipe over areas of concern with a gentle massage. Not recommended for diffusing.

Alternative oils: Massage Blend

"You did it!"
"No, you did it!"
"It wasn't me!"

The Digestive blend is known as the "tummy tamer." Peppermint, Ginger Oil and Anise seed all assist with reducing gas and bloating. Those oils combined with coriander seed, caraway seed, tarragon plant all aid in digestion and its occasional issues.

*Refer to dilution chart
Recommended application: 1 to 2 drops in the palm of your hand, lightly rub hands together and wipe over belly area. Tap the bottle on the large pads of your pet's back paws.

Alternative oils: Peppermint

"Oh yeah, that's the spot"

The use of massage in animals assists in balancing their systems and allows them to operate at their optimal level. Massage can decrease heart rate, enhance relaxation, and causes your pet's body to release endorphins, which are the bodies natural pain relievers. The combination of oils in the massage blend promote healthy circulation, help rid the body of toxins and reduce muscular tension. Cypress and Peppermint Oils are used to increase circulation and blood flow. Marjoram helps to soothe tense muscles and it was widely used by the Ancient Greeks and Romans. Peppermint also helps drive the oils in deeper, which allows them to work better.

*Refer to dilution chart
Recommended application: 1 or 2 drops in the palm of your hands, lightly rub your hands together, and gently massage areas of concern or use as an overall body massage. Excellent for senior dogs with creaky joints, dogs with an active lifestyle. This blend helps lessen tension for any anxious dog. Use this before and after activities to lessen muscle tension.

Alternative oils: Soothing Blend, Frankincense, Roman Chamomile, Peppermint

"No hitching a ride with me today fleas and ticks!

Cedarwood oil is used for several purposes. It naturally repels fleas and mosquitoes. Cedrol is a main chemical component of Cedarwood oil. It is often used in pest control products.

The ancient Egyptians used the oil in the embalming process, which in effect helped to keep the insects from disturbing the body. Additional uses of Cedarwood Oil are calming, promoting clear, healthy looking skin, while creating a relaxing environment.

*Refer to dilution chart when using topically
Recommended application: Apply 1 to 2 drops along the spine and belly. Place 1 to 2 drops in the palm of your hands and lightly rub together and wipe along spine and belly. Using a glass spray bottle, place 10 drops of Cedarwood in a 4 oz bottle, fill the rest with water. Shake well and spray on your pet's body. Refer to safety page, avoid spraying in their eyes. When you have active infestation do this 2 to 3 times a week. Doodle tip: For maintenance, spray them once a week. You can also spray their bedding area as well.

Alternative oils: Outdoor Blend

"A little privacy please! I am having digestive issues"

The Digestive Blend is a healthy, natural, and gentle way to soothe an upset stomach and settle feelings of motion sickness. This blend contains Ginger, Fennel, and Coriander which help ease stomach discomfort. Fennel is historically known to be used by in Chinese medicine and the Ancient Egyptians as food and digestive support. Ginger has been used in folk medicine for thousands of years to help with nausea and diarrhea. It also contains the plants peppermint, tarragon and caraway which assist in balancing a healthy digestive system.

*Refer to dilution chart
Recommended application: 1 to 2 drops applied directly on the belly area. Tapping bottle on the large pad on the back paws relieves symptoms as well. Excellent to have on hand when transporting for short or extended trips. This "tummy tamer" can be used as a preventative measure.

Alternative oils: Peppermint, Lavender, Frankincense

Glossary/Index

Melaleuca: Promotes healthy immune function, protects against seasonal and environmental threats, cleansing and rejuvenating effect on the skin.
Page: 35, 44, 47, 52

Outdoor Blend: Ylang Ylang Flower, Nootka Wood, Cedarwood Wood, Catnip, Lemon Eucalyptus, Litsea Fruit, Arborvitae Wood essential oils and Vanilla Bean absolute in a base of Fractionated Coconut Oil and Tamanu Seed Oil. Repels insects and environmental threats.
Page: 47, 50, 60

Peppermint: Aids in healthy respiratory function and clear breathing. Promotes healthy digestion and repels insects.
Page: 35, 38, 40, 47, 56, 58, 62

Protective Blend: Wild Orange Peel, Clove Bud, Cinnamon Bark/ Leaf, Eucalyptus Leaf, and Rosemary Leaf/ Flower essential oils. Supports healthy immune function.
Page: 35, 42

Reassuring Blend: Vetiver Root, Lavender Flower, Ylang Ylang Flower, Frankincense Resin, Clary Sage Flower, Marjoram Leaf, Labdanum Leaf/Stalk, Spearmint Herb. Promotes feelings of peace and relaxation, calming and grounding.
Page: 21, 22, 24, 28-32

Respiratory Blend: Laurel Leaf, Eucalyptus Leaf, Peppermint Plant, Melaleuca Leaf, Lemon Peel, Cardamom Seed, Ravintsara Leaf, Ravensara Leaf essential oils. Promotes clear breathing and minimizes seasonal threats.
Page: 35, 38, 40

Restful Blend: Lavender Flower, Cedarwood, Ho Wood Leaf, Ylang Ylang Flower, Marjoram Leaf, Roman Chamomile Flower, Vetiver Root, Vanilla Bean Absolute, Hawaiian Sandalwood Wood. Calming, grounding and relaxing, aids in restful sleep.
Page: 21-32, 36

Roman Chamomile: Calming effect on the skin, mind and body.
Page: 21-32, 36, 47, 48, 58

Soothing Blend: Wintergreen Leaf, Camphor Bark, Peppermint Plant, Ylang Ylang Flower, Helichrysum Flower, Blue Tansy Flower, Blue Chamomile Flower, and Osmanthus Flower. Soothes sore muscles and joints.
Page: 47, 48, 54, 58

Women's Blend: Bergamot Peel, Ylang Ylang Flower, Patchouli Leaf, Vanilla Bean Absolute, Jasmine Flower Absolute, Cinnamon Bark, Labdanum, Vetiver Root, Hawaiian Sandalwood, Cocoa Bean Absolute, Rose Flower essential oils in a base of Fractionated Coconut Oil. Calming and relaxing.
Page: 21, 24-32

References:

Ananda Apothecary - Eucalyptus Oil

Briggs P1,Hawrylack H, Mooney R. Nursing. 2016 Jul;46(7):61-7. Doi: 10.1097/01.NURSE.0000482882.38607.5c. Inhaled peppermint oil for postop nausea in patients undergoing cardiac surgery.

De Sousa AA, Soares PM, de Almeida AN, et al. Antispasmodic effect of Mentha piperita essential oil on tracheal smooth muscle of rats. J Ethnopharmacol. 2010;130(2):422-436.

Diaz JH1. Wilderness Environ Med. 2016 Mar;27(1):153-63. doi:10.1016/j.wem.2015.11.007. Epub 2016 Jan 27. Chemical and Plant-Based Insect Repellents:Efficacy, Safety, and Toxicity.

Doterratools.com

Elaissi A, Rouis Z, Salem NA, Mabrouk S, ben Salem Y, Salah KB, Aouni M, Farhat F, Chemli R, Harzallah-skhiri F, Khouja ML. Chemical composition of 8 eucalyptus species' essential oils and the evaluation of their antibacterial, antifungal and antiviral activities. BMC Complement Altern Med. 2012 Jun 28;12:81. Doi: 10.1186/1472-6882-12-81.

Eller F1, Vander Meer RK, Behle RW, Flor-Weiler LB, Palmquist DE. Environ Entomol. 2014 Jun;43(3):762-6. Doi: 10.1603/EN13270. Epub 2014 Mar 31. Bioactivity of cedarwood oil and cedrol against arthropod pests.

F Christopher, Kaulfers PM, Stahl Biskup E. A comparative study of the in vitro antimicrobial activity of tea tree oils s.l. With special reference to the activity of beta-triketones. Planta Med. 2000 Aug;66(6):556-60.

Frezzo, Mia and Jeremias, Jan (2014) Spoil Your Pet: a practical guide to using essential oils in dogs and cats

Gobel H1, Schmidt G, Dworschak M, Stolze H, Heuss D. Phytomedicine. 1995 Oct;2(2):93-102. Doi: 10.1016/S0944=7113(11)80053-X. Essential plant oils and headache mechanisms.

Health Benefit Times.com- Cardamom Oil

Hills, Jenny (2017) Healthy and Natural World

Hunt R1, Dienemann J, Norton H, Hartley W, Hudgens A, Stern T, Divine G. Anesth Analg. 2013 Sep;117(3):597-604. doi:10.1213/ANE.0b013e31824a0b1c. Epub 2012 Mar 5. Aromatherapy as treatment for postoperative nausea: a randomized trial.

J Ethnopharmacol. 2016 Feb 17;179 :22-6. Doi: 10.1016/j.jep.2015.12.039. Epub 2015 Dec 22. a-Pinene, linalool, and 1-octanol contribute to the topical anti-inflammatory and analgesic activities of frankincense by inhibiting COX-2.

J Mycol Med. 2014 Sep;24(3):234-40. Doi 10.1016/j.mycmed.2014.02.005. Epub 2014 Apr 17. Clinical and mycological evaluation of an herbal antifungal formulation in canine Malassezia dermatitis

Kim 1H1, Kim C, Seong K, Hur MH, Lim HM, Lee MS. Evid Based Complement Alternat Med. 2012;2012:984203.doi: 10.1155/2012/984203. Epub 2012 Nov 19. Essential oil inhalation on blood pressure and salivary cortisol levels in prehypertensive and hypertensive subjects.
Lans, C., Turner, N. & Khan, T. Parasitol Res (2008)103:889. doi:10.1007/s00436-008-1073-6

Medicinal plant treatments for fleas and ear problems of cats and dogs in British Columbia, Canada.

Lv YX1, Zhao SP, Zhang Y, Zhang H, Xie ZH, Cai GM, Jiang WH. Int J Biol Macromol. 2012 May 1;50(4):1144-50. Doi 10.1016/.ijbiomac.2012.02.002. Epub 2012 Feb 10. Effect of orange peel essential oil on oxidative stress in AOM animals.

New World Encyclopedia contributors (2008) newworldencyclopedia.org/p/index.php?title=Eucalyptus&oldid=79453

Organic Facts.net- Cardamom Oil

Perez-Roses R1, Risco E1,2, Vila R1, Penalver P3, Canigueral S1. J Agric Food Chem. 2016 Jun 15;64(23):4716-24. doi:10.1021/acs.jafc.6b00986. Epub 2016 Jun2. Biological and Nonbiological Antioxidant Activity of Some Essential Oils.
Perl O1, Arzi A1, Sela L1, Secundo L1, Holtzman Y1, Samnon P1, Oksenberg A2, Sobel N1, Hairston IS. J Neurophysiol.2016 May 1;115(5):2294-302. Doi: 10.1152/jn.01001.2015. Epub 2016 Feb 17. Odors enhance slow-wave activity in non rapid eye movement sleep.

Shelton, Melissa (2012) The Animal Desk Reference: Essential Oils for Animals

Shotola, Kim and Culver, Allison The Lightfoot Way

Srivastava JK, Shankar E, Gupta S. Chamomile: A herbal medicine of the past with bright future. Mol Med Rep. 2010; 3(6):895-901.

Wells DL. Aromatherapy for travel-induced excitement in dogs. J Am Vet Med Assoc.2006;229(6)964-967.

Wilson, Sabrina (2017) Organic Daily Post - Cedar Oil

"Keep your eyes peeled for more adventures with Doodle and his pals as they explore the world of essential oils and all their uses."

28102133R00042

Made in the USA
Lexington, KY
10 January 2019